THE WORLD OF MYTHOLOGY:
EGYPTIAN MYTHOLOGY

BY JIM OLLHOFF

VISIT US AT
WWW.ABDOPUBLISHING.COM

Published by ABDO Publishing Company, 8000 West 78th Street, Suite 310, Edina, MN 55439. Copyright ©2011 by Abdo Consulting Group, Inc. International copyrights reserved in all countries. No part of this book may be reproduced in any form without written permission from the publisher. ABDO & Daughters™ is a trademark and logo of ABDO Publishing Company.

Printed in the United States of America, North Mankato, Minnesota.
112010
012011

Editor: John Hamilton
Graphic Design: Sue Hamilton
Cover Design: Neil Klinepier
Cover Photo: Gonzalo Ordóñez
Interior Photos and Illustrations: Alamy-pg 28; AP-pgs 9, 10 & 14; Corbis-pgs 11, 16, 17, 20 & 26; Getty Images-pgs 7, 15, 19, 21, 24, 27 & 29; Granger Collection-pgs 22 & 23; iStockphoto-pgs 5, 8, 26 & 29; Photo Researchers-pgs 12 & 13; Thinkstock-pg 25; University of Wisconsin-Milwaukee-pg 4.

Library of Congress Cataloging-in-Publication Data

Ollhoff, Jim, 1959-
    Egyptian mythology / Jim Ollhoff.
        p. cm. -- (The world of mythology)
    ISBN 978-1-61714-719-7
    1. Mythology, Egyptian--Juvenile literature. I. Title.
    BL2441.3.O45 2011
    398.20932--dc22
                                    2010032584

CONTENTS

THE MIGHTY MYTH

Why does the moon seem to change its shape throughout the month? Why are there shiny little lights in the night sky? Why does the sun rise every single morning no matter what? Where does the sun go at night?

Throughout history, people have looked up at the sky and wondered what it all meant. The events of the sky are so grand and glorious that they remind us of sacred things. Ever since people have been around, they have been telling stories about why the moon, stars, and sky behave the way they do. Most early cultures of the world had a "god of the sky" who caused all the things to

Above: The Egyptian god Ra.

happen. The Egyptians had several sky gods. The most famous sky god was named Ra.

The word "myth" comes from the Greek word *mythos*, which means "story." Myths are stories that people invented to explain why the sun rises and sets, why the moon and stars act like they do, and other mysteries of life. Other myths told stories that helped people know how to act, or gave comfort to people during hard times. The sharing of myths has always been, and always will be, part of what it means to be human.

Above: A crescent moon in Egypt. Throughout history, people wondered why the moon changed shape and where the sun went at night. Stories were created to explain why the moon, stars, and sky behave the way they do.

LAND OF THE PYRAMIDS

Above: According to legend, King Menes united lower and upper Egypt in about 3150 BC. After that, Egypt became a powerful country.

One of the oldest civilizations on Earth is Egypt. According to legend, a King named Menes united the country in about 3150 BC. After that, Egypt became a powerful country. It was ruled by pharaohs, or kings. These pharaohs were sometimes worshiped as gods.

Egypt's most important natural resource is the Nile River. The Nile begins deep in Africa and flows northward through low-lying lands to the Mediterranean Sea. Egyptians have relied on the Nile for irrigation and drinking water for thousands of years. Through the centuries, most of the population of Egypt has lived near the Nile, where the river's water creates fertile soil for crops. Much of the rest of the country is desert.

Construction of the pyramids near the city of Giza was started during a time called the Old Kingdom, beginning in 2686 BC. Pyramids were giant tombs for the pharaohs.

Above: Construction of the pyramids near the city of Giza, Egypt, was started in about 2686 BC. Pyramids were giant tombs for the pharaohs.

THE SOUL OF EGYPT

The Egyptian god Seth.

Egyptians have told mythological stories for thousands of years. However, they only began writing them down in about 2000 BC. The ancient Egyptians had thousands of gods. People in every region had their own gods, their own myths, and their own temples. As people from different regions began to mix, the stories began to blend together. Gods from one area were included in myths from other areas.

The Egyptians were perfectly happy with different, overlapping myths. They didn't have a single, unified myth story. Sometimes the myths contradicted each other. For example, in one set of stories, the god Seth is the protector of southern Egypt. In other stories, he's the enemy of all the gods.

Some myths were stories that gave people lessons in life. In one such story, the goddess Isis dressed herself as a poor woman to see who would help her. A rich woman saw Isis, but refused to help her. However, a poor fisherman's wife saw Isis and took her in. Scorpions stung the rich woman as punishment for not helping Isis. In her sorrow, the rich woman gave all her belongings to the fisherman's wife. This story illustrates the importance of generosity and human caring.

Above: Queen Nefertari (left), wife of Pharaoh Ramses II, is led to the afterlife by the goddess Isis (right). Isis was one of Egypt's greatest goddesses, a protector and a mother.

Above: The Egyptian gods Anubis (jackel's head), Thoth (ibis's head), and Ammut (crocodile head).

The early Egyptians believed that every animal had a spirit. Most gods and goddesses were pictured with a human body and the head of an animal or bird, and the god took the spirit of that animal. For example, the goddess Ammut had the head of a crocodile to show that she was cold-hearted and scary.

Over time, the stories of the gods changed. A few of the gods and myths became very popular with all Egyptians. Some of the most popular included Ra, the sun god. Osiris was the good god of the underworld. Osiris's wife, Isis, was the goddess of motherhood and protector of children. Isis became such a popular goddess that she was later included in Greek and Roman myths. In ancient Rome, Isis became the queen of heaven.

Above: Osiris, the god of the underworld.

CREATION

Creation myths are stories about how the world began. Different regions of Egypt had different creation myths. In the city of Thebes, the sun god Amon-Ra was the first god, and he created all other gods. In the city of Memphis, the god Ptah, the god of crafts, built all the other gods out of gold and other metals. On Elephantine Island, Khnum, the god of the Nile, made humans out of clay.

Probably the most popular creation myth came from the city of Heliopolis. The story begins with a giant ocean, a watery chaos called Nun. The sun god Atum emerged from the watery chaos and created two children. Shu was the god of the air, and Tefenet was the goddess of the water. Shu and Tefenet went to explore the land. They were gone so long that Atum began to worry. When they finally came back, he wept for joy. Atum's tears became the first humans.

Shu and Tefenet had two children. Geb was the earth god, and Nut was the sky goddess. Geb and Nut fell in love. But when they embraced, there was no space between them. Their father Shu, the god of the air, separated them. He put Nut high up in the sky, and Geb on the earth below. With the sky and stars above, and the earth below, people had room to live.

Left: Shu the air god (center) raises Nut the sky goddess (blue, forming the arch of the sky) to separate her from Geb the earth god (across bottom).

Above: The ram-headed god Khnum, guardian of the source of the Nile, was said to have made humans out of clay on Elephantine Island.

THE SUN GOD

The sun god was one of the main gods of ancient Egypt. He was most frequently called "Ra," or "Re." Two different gods were sometimes put together and referred to as one god. Ra was combined with Amon, a fertility god who was worshiped in Thebes. He became known as Amon-Ra. Atum, another creator god, was added to Ra and became known as Atum-Ra. This kind of god-fusion was common in Egyptian mythology.

Ra, the sun god, would make his way across the sky each day. Sometimes he is pictured as a dung beetle. Dung beetles rolled balls of dung across the ground, just like Ra rolled the sun across the sky.

One of the stories said that Ra was born every morning, got older every afternoon, and was very old by sundown. He traveled through the underworld all night and was born again in the morning. The early Egyptian people worshiped Ra and performed rituals so that he would continue to bring the sunlight each day.

Above: Ra, the sun god, makes his way across the sky each day.

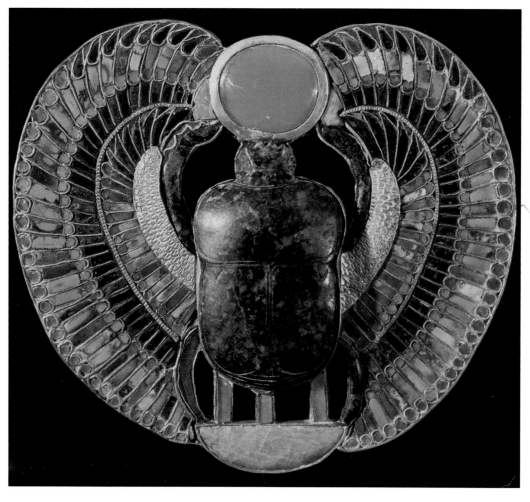

Above: Egyptian jewelry depicting a scarab beetle with the sun. *Below:* A dung beetle.

The Origin of Death and Disease

The ancient Egyptians had several myths about how death and disease first came to the world. One of the myths included the aging sun god Ra.

Ra had become bored with the people of the world. The people realized that Ra had abandoned them, so they began worshiping other gods. This angered Ra, so he ordered the fierce goddess Sekhmet to kill everyone. Sekhmet had the head of a lion. She was so severe that her breath alone destroyed Egypt's vegetation and turned the land into a desert. Sekhmet began to destroy humanity.

However, Ra changed his mind when he saw all the violence. He couldn't make Sekhmet stop, because she was in a terrible killing frenzy. So, Ra got 7,000 jars of beer and dyed it red so that it looked like blood. Sekhmet drank the beer, fell asleep, and forgot about killing people. Humanity was saved, but now violence, disease, and death were a part of the world.

Ra decided to leave the world, but first he decided to help the people. He created Thoth, the moon god, so that people could have light at night and wouldn't be afraid. Then he made the good and wise god Osiris to be the new king of the world.

Thoth, the moon god.

Above: The fierce goddess Sekhmet had the head of a lion. She was sent to earth by the sun god Ra to kill all humans. Her breath alone was said to have destroyed all of Egypt's vegetation, turning the land into a desert.

THE GOOD KING OSIRIS

As king of the world and the god of agriculture, Osiris taught people how to plant crops and farm the land. Isis, his wife and sister, ruled at his side. It was a golden age for people and their gods.

But Osiris' brother Seth was very jealous. Seth wanted Osiris' throne so he could be king. Seth killed Osiris. However, Isis used her magic to keep his body from decaying. Isis, together with the jackal-god Anubis, mummified Osiris. Osiris then became the god of the underworld, the place that holds all the souls of dead people.

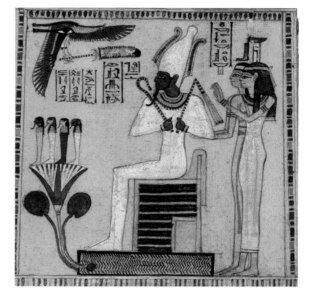

Above: Osiris sits in front of his wife, Isis, and her sister, Nephthys. After Osiris died, he became the god of the underworld.

Isis and her sister Nephthys mourned Osiris. They are often pictured as sparrow hawks, grieving over Osiris. In fact, at ancient Egyptian funerals, two women often dressed as Isis and Nephthys, mourning for the deceased person.

Above: Anubis, the jackal-headed god of mummification and protector of tombs.

Above: Horus, the falcon god and son of Isis and Osiris, became the rightful king over Seth, Osiris's brother.

Isis gave birth to a son, Horus, who was the rightful new king. Isis, however, knew that Seth would try to kill Horus, too.

Finally, Isis and Horus went to a tribunal of the gods, a court where they might find justice. The gods heard the testimony of Seth to see if his claim to the throne was worthy. Seth told the gods that only he was strong enough to keep the sun rising each day. They argued and argued, and couldn't come to a decision. Then they had a series of contests between Seth and Horus, but they still couldn't come to a decision.

Finally, from his home in the underworld, Osiris wrote a letter to the tribunal of the gods. Osiris said that if they didn't make Horus the new king, he would send demons and monsters from the underworld to the homes of the gods. All the gods quickly agreed that Horus should be the new king.

Above: Offerings are made to Egyptian demons. Osiris threatened to send demons and monsters from the underworld if his son, Horus, was not made king.

MUMMIES AND THE AFTERLIFE

The ancient Egyptians believed that when a person died, the spirit left the body and went to the underworld. Once in the underworld, the person's spirit had to travel a long distance, and face many dangers, before finding his or her body again. They hoped that their spirit could be reunited with their body so they could spend time with the good god Osiris, king of the underworld. They hoped that they could eventually reach the boat of the sun god Ra, which would take them to the Field of Reeds, a happy paradise.

But first, the dead person's spirit had to travel through the underworld, which was a place of deserts, fires, islands, and crocodiles. Luckily, there was a how-to manual that helped them navigate the dangers of the underworld. It was a collection of advice called *The Book of the Dead*.

Above: The Barge of the Sun sails through the underworld.

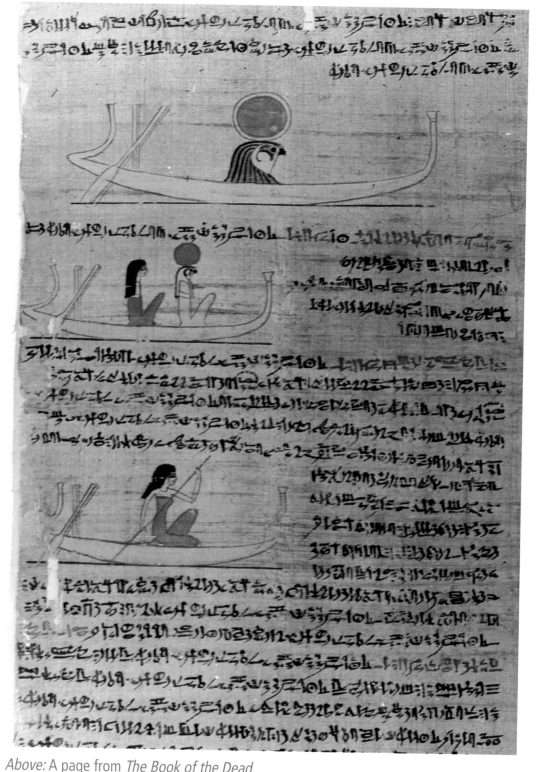

Above: A page from *The Book of the Dead.*

Once the disembodied spirit made it through the underworld, it had to link back up with its body. First, the spirit had to find the body. That's why a person's likeness was painted on the outside of his or her coffin. The likeness helped the spirit recognize its own body. Hopefully, the family and friends of the deceased mummified the body. A mummified body was better preserved, so that the spirit could more easily reconnect with it in the underworld.

Left: In ancient Egypt, a person's likeness was painted on the outside of his or her sarcophagus, or coffin. The likeness was believed to help the person's spirit recognize its own body in the afterlife.

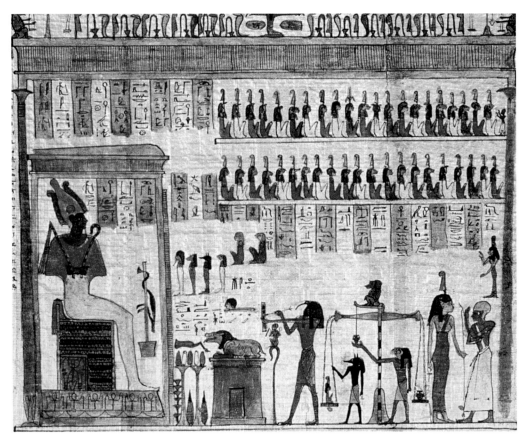

Above: The weighing of a person's heart (middle right). Only good people were permitted into the Field of Reeds. Bad people were eaten by the Devourer of the Dead.

The final test was in Osiris's throne room. Osiris wanted to know if the person was good or bad. Only good people were permitted into the Field of Reeds. The person stood in front of a scale. Maat, the goddess of justice, put feathers on one side of the scale. The person's heart was put on the other side. The heart of a good person would be as light as a feather, which was revealed by the scale. The heart of a bad person, however, would be heavy with evil, and tip the scale. In that case, a monster called the Devourer of the Dead would leap out and eat the bad person.

OTHER GODS AND GODDESSES

Bastet, the goddess of war.

The list of Egyptian gods goes on and on. Many gods were shown as animals, or had animal heads. Bastet, the goddess of war and later the goddess of love, was portrayed as a cat. Thoth, the scribe of the gods, was often shown with the head of an ibis or sometimes a baboon. Hathor, the goddess of motherhood, was often pictured as a cow.

Above: The gods Horus (hawk), ruler of the living, Tawaret (hippo), goddess of fertility and childbirth, and Hathor (cow), goddess of motherhood.

Kings, or pharaohs, often considered themselves to be divine incarnations of Ra or Horus. Others saw themselves as sons of Osiris and Isis. Some kings were considered divine after they were dead. Other kings, such as Amenhotep III, proclaimed themselves divine as soon as they took the throne.

Egypt is home to more than 90 pyramids. These pyramids were tombs for the pharaohs. Rooms in the pyramids were stocked with food, household articles, chariots, and even dead servants, so that the pharaohs could use those items in the underworld.

Above: A replica of some of the items found in King Tutankhamun's tomb. Food, beds, chariot, chairs, and many other items were left for the pharaoh's use in the afterlife.

Magic

In ancient Egypt, the purpose of magic was to get the gods to do what you wanted. Sometimes magic was in the form of an amulet, which might protect the wearer from harm. Sometimes magic was meant to help in times of trouble. *The Book of the Dead* helped spirits get through the dangerous underworld. Some magic spells could even make hearts appear weightless, which was useful when Osiris weighed hearts to find out if they were evil.

Priests studied magic books, so people began to believe they could do amazing things. One story tells of a priest who made a wax crocodile, which came to life to kill someone the priest didn't like. Some priests, it was said, could tame lions or cure diseases.

Ancient Egyptians lived in a very spiritual world, and so magic made sense to them. In a land full of gods and goddesses, magic was like a map that helped people find their way around.

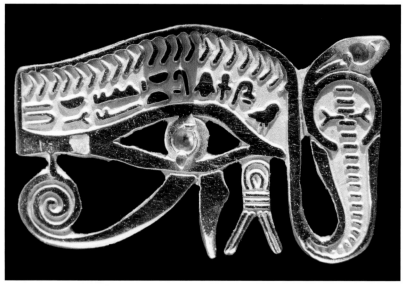

Left: An Eye of Horus (god of the sky) amulet. Sometimes, magic in the form of an amulet was thought to protect the wearer from harm.

Above: Pharoah Ramses offers incense to the god Amun. In ancient Egypt, the purpose of magic was to get the gods to do what you wanted.

Nut   Shu   Tefenet   Geb   Isis   Anubis   Hathor   Thoth   Saf   Seback

Above: A few of the many gods and goddesses that ancient Egyptians relied on to help them in their day-to-day lives.

GLOSSARY

AMULET

A charm used to ward off evil or bring good fortune.

ANUBIS

The jackel-headed god of mummification and protector of tombs.

The Egyptian god Anubis.

BOOK OF THE DEAD

An ancient Egyptian book containing prayers, magic, hymns, and instructions on what the soul of a dead person should do on his or her trip through the afterlife.

CREATION MYTHS

Stories about how the world began. In ancient Egypt, different regions had different creation myths. For example, people in the city of Thebes believed the sun god Amon-Ra was the first god, and he created all other gods.

DECAY

A process that happens after death when a body begins to rot, breaking down into its most basic elements.

Field of Reeds

The paradise where good people go when they die.

Isis

The wife and sister of Osiris.

Mummification

A process where most of the water has been removed from an animal or human body. Mummification retains the body's shape and preserves it for a long period of time.

Nile

The River Nile, which flows through central and eastern Egypt.

Osiris

The god of the underworld.

Pharaoh

The title given to the rulers, or kings, of ancient Egypt.

Ra

The sun god.

Underworld

A dark, dangerous place through which Egyptians believed the dead must travel in order to reach the afterlife.

INDEX

The Egyptian god Horus.